Free Verse Editions

Edited by Jon Thompson

THE MAGNETIC BRACKETS

Jesús Losada

Translated by Michael Smith and Luis Ingelmo

Parlor Press
Anderson, South Carolina
www.parlorpress.com

Parlor Press LLC, Anderson, South Carolina, 29621

Printed in the United States of America
S A N: 2 5 4 - 8 8 7 9

Library of Congress Cataloging-in-Publication Data

Losada, Jesús, 1962-
[Paréntesis imantados. English]
The magnetic brackets / Jesús Losada ; translated by Michael Smith and Luis Ingelmo.
pages cm
"... from the original Spanish language version Los parentesis imantados by Jesus Losada."
ISBN 978-1-60235-606-1 (pbk. : alk. paper)
I. Smith, Michael, 1942 September 1- translator. II. Ingelmo, Luis, translator. III. Title.
PQ6662.O815P3713 2012
861'.64--dc23

2014045409

Cover design by David Blakesley
Cover photo by Patrik Goethe. Used by permission from Unsplash. com.

1 2 3 4 5

Printed on acid-free paper.

Parlor Press, LLC is an independent publisher of scholarly and trade titles in print and multimedia formats. This book is available in paperback and ebook formats from Parlor Press on the World Wide Web at http://www.parlorpress.com or through online and brick-and-mortar bookstores. For submission information or to find out about Parlor Press publications, write to Parlor Press, 3015 Brackenberry Drive, Anderson, South Carolina, 29621, or email editor@parlorpress.com.

For Carmen Isla. For Marcial Sánchez—
Time, just time.

For José Miguel Martín Juárez (1961-1996)—
Beauty & death.

For Claudio Rodríguez (1934-1999),
who was so close to these lines.

Foreword

A Book of Maturity

I recall, as if it were just now, the day the first book of Jesús Losada came into my hands. It was *Indulgencia plenaria* (Plenary Indulgence) published by Gramma in Madrid, during 1992. I recall that reading because for me these were difficult days and those poems allowed me a taste of tranquility and profundity. I found myself, quite simply, before a persuasive and moving book. It was no small matter back then, when poetry tended towards hollowness and flatness, lacking in content, confined to 'photographing' reality in shades of gray.

Later, other books came that confirmed that first voice heading for depth, to what is *beyond*, in books such as *Huerto cerrado del amor* (Love's Walled Garden) which achieved being shortlisted for the Premio Adonáis in 1994.

Afterwards came *Novenario* (Novena) in 1997, illustrated by Javier Carpintero.

And a new book, winner of the classic "Provincia" of León in 1998: *La noche del funambulista* (The Tightrope Walker's Night).

This book opened up in the poetry Jesús Losada another tone, without rejecting what was his essential voice, that which seeks the human above all else. With this book there were changes in his poetry, some related to his experiences, to his display of the ocean of Portugal, in works such as *Tu rostro en el agua de otra manera* (Your Face On The Water In A Different Way) with drawings by the painter Toño Barreiro, a work of the year 2000. Also the very atmospheric book—due to the accompanying, beautiful images of the Portuguese photographer Daniel Curval—with the title *Hombre desnudo persignándose en azul* (A Naked Man Crossing Himself In Blue), a Spanish/Portuguese bilingual edition of 2001.

In the apparent contradiction of this title there rests a good deal of the truth of this poet who looks at the world and at his inner self with equal passion, with the same desire of revealing secrets through his creative adventure.

This "Atlantic cycle or oceanic phase" closes with his last book of 2003, titled *Cuaderno Atlántico* (Atlantic Notebook).

Over time I have later had the good fortune to enjoy the friendship of this Brother Poet and to follow more closely his vital enthusiasm, his creative restlessness. That said, one will understand with what satisfaction I write now these introductory words for his recent, new book, *Los paréntesis imantados* (The Magnetic Brackets).

I have read and reread it calmly and have had the opportunity of reaffirming that sensation which the reading of his first book produced in me: the simple and plain sensation that, quite simply, we are before a poet of such great authenticity, fated to sing with a very necessary voice in a difficult time.

Beyond all possible changes, we again encounter in this book by Jesús Losada, his perennial dialogue with the *sacred*.

This is what I mean: a dialogue with that same gaze of acceptance and piety thrown over the reality that metamorphoses the world.

The sacred—a presence, assuredly, rather unorthodox—is then a reality that only the language of the poet can enrich or salvage, acquiring with it the word, the character of an *illuminating* revelation.

It was necessary to make this preliminary clarification, to allude to this constant fidelity of his voice to a sacred reality, to say later what this book is specifically characterized by. A book, fundamentally, of love.

But also we would be wrong if we were to give this word a sense that would be hackneyed or trite. The word "love" has, as we know, multiple meanings, but in this book it is refined, since love-passion trembles in these pages, indeed, with an extreme delicacy; and, at the same time, another love even more subtle—Dante alluded to it, at the end of his Paradise, as a love that can move the *Sole e l'altre stelle*—deepens and re-enforces the whole overall message of the book.

The years have passed for this author and, without abandoning his previous essential voice, his language has been compressed, it has become more precise. There is not, for certain, in the poems on the following pages, any spare word or expression out of place.

We are, then, before a book of maturity; before a book in which the fullness of being and writing is offered to us in a very emphatic way.

Jesús Losada—going against the current of the poetry which was imposed on us in these last two decades—has limited himself to *sowing*, to maintaining his voice and now harvests that best fruit, that of seeing his message grown and perfected.

Time passes. The gaze calms down. What first was in the poetry of Losada an intention, an ideation, an investigation, is now a true certainty.

I am willing to quote here some lines or paragraphs, but I hesitate to do so since it would seem to upset the achieved unity, the secret of this book which has no spare words, as we said before.

The pleasure of reading and re-reading is imposed. The book even withstands the test of opening it at any page, of approaching it at any stanza, or of reading just one of its lines.

We are, Losada says, "asleep / under the blade of a jackknife" and we know that, at times, it is "a bunch of hawthorns" we breathe in the night of being and non-being, but beyond the threat is that temperance of he who knows he has sought out and found.

Every "black ending" will be thus a beginning: hope.

The Magnetic Brackets, accordingly, is one of the liveliest and truest poetical testaments that a reader can tackle at these times of disbelief, of half-truths, of vacuity and passivity in thought. For this is one more gift from the book: where thought and feeling are perfectly merged.

The shakings of the world may keep coming, but "the flames of the candles" will keep on burning with their temperance; since in the end everything "will be the dream of a dream." A dream—that of the creator—come true.

In his first book Jesús Losada went out there to live his truth, to live his adventure, an *inner adventure*. From this adventure he emerged unscathed and with the gem of some lines that no future time will undo.

Antonio Colinas
Salamanca, April 2007

First Lines

Cum subit illius tristissima noctis imago.

—*Ovid*

But in the end the most bitter dawn will arrive
taking along this dream
of the white setting fire to the white.

—*Antonio Colinas*

Na longa noite que hoje começa
acendi a candeia que alumia o caminho
da tua alma.

—*José Agostinho Baptista*

THE MAGNETIC BRACKETS

Aquellos lados del invierno
lentamente húmedos.

Encalados
serenamente tristes, fríos.

Noche tras noche
esperando
siempre en silencio.

Las ventanas cerradas
y la vida dentro.

La vida dentro la vida.

Those sides of winter
slowly moist.

Whitewashed
calmly sorrowful, cold.

Night after night
always
waiting in silence.

The windows closed
and life inside.

Life inside, life.

La noche.

Esa araña negra que nos atrapaba
con sus quelíceros
y succionaba
nuestros jugos adormecidos
dejando exhaustos
nuestros cuerpos
de insectos devorados.

La entrega mortal
del veneno
entre los labios.

The night.

That black spider that trapped us
with its chelicerae
and sucked
our drowsy juices
leaving our bodies,
devoured by insects,
exhausted.

The fatal yielding
of poison
between our lips.

Somos hombres de fechas.
Hojas arrancadas al santoral.

El ovillo de los años
deslizándose
entre los dedos.

¿No son los fríos nuestra mejor geometría?

Un abrazo infinito.
Nuestras bocas apretadas
para llegar
a la despedida del estío.

Una ceremonia de lagartijas
reptando
por un derretido muro de leche.

Las golondrinas en hilera
sobre un cable de alta tensión.

Antes de emigrar
picotean sus vientres.
Buscan entre sus alas
la ceniza de un despojo
… o el tesoro
más alto del vuelo.

We are made out of dates.
Leaves torn from the calendar.

The yarn-ball of the years
slipping
through one's fingers.

Aren't these colds our best geometry?

An infinite embrace.
Our mouths pressing
to reach
the summer's farewell.

A ceremony of wall lizards
slithering
on a melted wall of milk.

Swallows in line
on a high-tension wire.

Before migrating
they peck their bellies.
They look in their wings
for the ashes of a dispossession
… or for the loftiest
treasure of flight.

Los trillos abandonados
a la puerta de los establos.
Ollas para la manteca
y cántaros de vino, rotos
detrás de las tapias de adobe
junto a los aperos de labranza.

El hilo eterno de las ruecas
duerme, como las reses,
el sueño plácido del heno
bajo un dintel
con signos de cantero.

La existencia envejece
a la luz del carburo.

La existencia envejece
a la sombra del sacrificio.

The threshers abandoned
at the gate of the stables.
Pots for the butter
and pitchers of wine, broken
behind the adobe walls
beside the farm tools.

The eternal thread of the distaffs
sleeps, like the cows,
the peaceful sleep of hay
under a lintel
with mason marks.

Existence grows old
by the light of the carbide lamp.

Existence grows old
in the shadow of the sacrifice.

Hemos grabado con cincel
en el arco de las constelaciones
el palpitar de nuestras horas oscuras.

La ceniza de sus aristas.

La cúpula más gris del invierno.

We engraved with chisel
on the arch of the constellations
the pulsing of our dark hours.

The ash of their edges.

The grayer dome of winter.

El temblor de mis manos
era entonces
el temblor más anciano de sus manos
cuando sujetaban una hogaza de pan
dándole concavidad
con un cuchillo.

Sobre el mandil de la vejez
caían las migas
como alimento para el hambre.

Y el regreso blanco nunca más fue posible.

Mi memoria es hoy
escarcha
en el círculo
del corazón.

The trembling of my hands
was then
the most ancient trembling of their hands
when they held a loaf of bread
turning it concave
with a knife.

On the apron of old age
crumbs fell
like food for hunger.

And the white return was never possible again.

My memory is today
frost
on the circle
of my heart.

Llegan de lejos.

Vienen ofreciendo silencio
todo el silencio
áspero en sus manos.

Mientras nosotros
tallamos sobre este relámpago de piedra
nombres
que perdieron su identidad
en el bosque de la leyenda.

They arrive from afar.

They come offering silence
all the silence
harsh in their hands.

Meanwhile we
carve on this stone lightning
names
that lost their identity
in the woods of legend.

Aún recuerdo

algunas noches de fúnebre réquiem
de incienso
de esquila muda o campana difunta
encordándonos la vida.

Nada más entrar me descalzaba.
Dejaba mis botas de cuero
al lado de tus zapatos,
junto a tu ropa santa de seda y nácar.

Descalzos ascendíamos
para llegar
desnudos
hasta la cumbre
por tortuosos senderos de zarzas.

Y la nieve en la lengua
nos abrasaba de amor.

Ungiéndonos con óleo nocturno
semilla fértil para la tierra.

Cuando llegaba la mañana
escuchábamos el jadear del gozo
respirando su olor
su sudor
nos alimentábamos de la pureza
que nos entregaban las sombras
y ocupaban nuestro territorio.

Las horas
eran el bostezo luminoso del sueño.

I still remember

some nights of funereal requiem
of incense
of a mute convent bell or a deceased toll
knelling our lives.

On entering I would bare my feet.
I would leave my leather boots
right by your shoes,
near your holy clothes of silk and nacre.

Barefoot we would ascend
to reach
naked
the top
through winding paths full of brambles.

And the snow on our tongue
scorched us with love.

Anointed with night oils,
fertile seed for the soil.

When morning broke
we heard the panting of delight
smelling its scent
of sweat
we fed on the purity
the shadows cast on us
while occupying our territory.

The hours
were the luminous yawn of sleep.

Fue el amor.

Un amor que bebimos
hasta saciar nuestra sed
de dioses agotados.

El cáliz vacío.

Y ahora me pregunto

¿qué nos queda?

…

It was love.

A love we drank
until satiating our thirst
for exhausted gods.

The empty chalice.

And now I wonder,

What's left to us?

…

Las agujas del reloj hirviendo
como navajas afiladas
que cortaban las venas del amor

–un amor entre sueños–

Instante de eternidad.

Seguir
por el alambre interminable
del viaje
antiguo de la noche.

Pero el tiempo
era azufre en los ojos
cianuro con el café
y galletas rancias de amargura.

The hands of the clock boiling
like sharp jackknives
that cut the veins of love—

a love amid dreams—

An eternal instant.

To walk on,
on the infinite tightrope
of night's old
trip.

But time
was sulfur in our eyes,
cyanide in our coffee
and stale cookies of sorrow.

Fuera de la habitación
el invierno temblaba de frío.

La eyaculada carne de nuestros cuerpos.

No cuentes las horas.

Su tiempo
es la soga que ahorca
nuestro destino.

Outside the room
winter shuddered with cold.

The ejaculated flesh of our bodies.

Don't count the hours.

Their time
is the rope that chokes
our fate.

Llueve
sobre las piedras de cuarzo.

Llanto que moja suave
la sequedad del alma.

Anoche
apenas quedaban hojas en los árboles.

Cayeron
al suelo del jardín
los nidos de los gorriones.

Todo permanecía desnudo.

Pasó el viento.

La tristeza
pertenece a este rincón del mundo.

Nosotros somos los huéspedes
que alquilamos sus habitaciones.

Pero…
¿al otro lado de la calle continúa existiendo la vida?

It is raining
on the quartz stones.

Tears that softly wet
the soul's dryness.

Last night
the trees were almost leafless.

The sparrow nests
fell down
to the yard.

Everything was bare.

The wind passed by.

Sorrow
belongs in this corner of the world.

We are the guests
renting its rooms.

But …
is there still life on the other side of the street?

… Fuera del mundo

–amor–
las horas
bordan con hilo de plata
(dentro del templo)
cuerpos zurcidos
a la candidez de la sábana.

Algodón en alcobas
que huelen a limpio
dulce azúcar blanco.

Y la noche
tiene la velocidad lenta de los sentidos.

Manera única de perpetuarnos
de ser.

De ser.

… Outside the world—

love—
the hours
hem with silver thread
(inside the church)
darned bodies
to the candor of the sheet.

Cotton in alcoves
that smell like clean
sweet white sugar.

And night
has the slow speed of the senses.

A unique manner of enduring,
of being.

Of being.

Siempre hay una víspera
para la partida
que nunca llega.

El equipaje espera vacío.

Armarios llenos de añoranza
con sus jerséis de lana gruesa
y el olor litúrgico de las bolas de alcanfor
colgadas en las perchas.

Hay membrillos en los cajones maduros
de sábanas almidonadas.

Un tiempo que nos invade
como una polilla
y nos sobrevuela
inútilmente
en silencio.

There is always an eve
of the departure
that never arrives.

The baggage awaits empty.

Closets full of yearning
with thick wool sweaters
and the liturgical smell of mothballs
hanging from the hangers.

In the drawers there are quinces ripe
with starched sheets.

A time that invades us
like a clothes moth
and flies over us
uselessly,
quietly.

Ya entonces éramos
y rezábamos
nuestra plegaria carnal
con interminables jaculatorias
desgranando rosarios
de besos sobre la piel anaranjada
donde ardía la cera de la noche.

La penitencia era el amor.

Su fragancia
el cuaresmal aroma de los lirios morados.

Back then we already were
and prayed
our carnal orison
with endless ejaculatory prayers
telling and threshing rosaries
of kisses on the orangy skin
where the wax of night burned.

Penance was love.

Its scent
the Lenten aroma of purple lilies.

En la mesilla de nogal
la pera de la luz
un vaso con agua
y cáscaras secas de fruta.
Un plato de porcelana esborcellada
sirve de cenicero, las colillas amontonadas
y una caja de fósforos
para iluminar el rostro
del que se sabe perseguido.

He amado tantas horas
junto a tu cuerpo
que te escribiría kilómetros de astros.

Una caligrafía de estrellas
cerrando los párpados
de tus ojos fatigados.

Guardaría en un arca el luto
que se aproxima lento
a tus heridas.

La llaga escondida en tu costado.

In the walnut nightstand
the light switch
a glass of water
and dry fruit peels.
A chipped porcelain plate
used as an ashtray, cigarette butts piling up
and a box of matches
to light up the face
of him who knows himself chased down.

I have loved for so many hours
by your body
that I would write miles of stars for you.

A calligraphy of heavenly bodies
on closing the lids
of your exhausted eyes.

I'd put away in a chest the mourning
that is slowly drawing close
to your wounds.

The hidden stigma on your side.

Amor
hoy no hay horizonte
para ver el vuelo negro
de los vencejos,
ni las bandadas de la muerte.

Nos hemos mirado
y apareció más noche.

Te he palpado
con la yema de mis dedos
con la azada que cubre mi boca

y eres hermosa y desconocida.

My love,
there is no horizon today
to watch the black flight
of the swifts,
or the flocks of death.

We have looked at each other
and a deeper night has come over us.

I have felt you
with my fingertips
with the hoe covering my mouth

and you are beautiful and unknown.

En ti
está toda mi vida y la ausencia.

Secretos como espadas
cortando
el hilo invisible de los silencios
en ciegas noches de perdido equilibrista.

Sin dirección.

Camino
trazando circunferencias,
líneas, geografías
y lugares inexistentes.

Para reposar al final
sobre lechos compartidos de espinas.

Amor

eres la medida del abandono.

El ángel
que abre sus alas
blancas en esta oscuridad
–que es todo–
y flagela las meninges de mi pensamiento.

In you
is all my life and absence.

Secrets like swords
cutting
the invisible thread of silences
in blind nights of a lost tightrope walker.

Directionless.

I walk
tracing circumferences,
lines, geographies
and non-existent places.

To rest finally
on shared beds of thorns.

Love

you are the measure of abandonment.

The angel
that opens its wings
white in this darkness—
which is everything—
and scourges the meninges of my thought.

Presagio el fin
entre estas cuatro paredes
austeras y desnudas
como la estricta soledad
de un vientre vacío
sin alimento.

I foresee the end
amid these four walls
austere and naked
like the strict solitude
of an empty belly
without food.

… Llegan de lejos.

Vienen
con la muerte en sus arterias
con flores negras creciendo en la médula.

Apostando por la vida
con billetes sucios, manoseados.

Vienen
subidos al lomo turbio de los caballos
galopando
con el sueño de ser otros.

Incendiando antorchas
amapolas
gritando sangre y bruma
con ronca voz de opio
sobre el tumor de la noche.

… They arrive from afar.

They come
with death in their arteries
with black flowers growing in their marrow.

Betting on life
with dirty, worn banknotes.

They come
astride the horses' murky backs
galloping
with dreams of being someone else.

Burning torches
poppies
shouting blood and mist
with a hoarse opium voice
over the tumor of night.

Son ellos.

Los reconocemos
envueltos en lágrimas ajenas.

En banderas
de viento.

Buscando el norte.

Con su brújula de invierno
a la intemperie.

It’s them.

We recognize them
enveloped in the tears of others.

In flags
of wind.

Finding their bearings.

With their winter compass
out in the open.

Pero no, aún es temprano.

Y en la penumbra de esta habitación
que duerme y sueña
con nosotros,
respira la luz del alba
filtrándose
por las rendijas de la persiana
al clarear.

Dándole nombre a los objetos: perchero,
bombilla, crucifijo, libros… espejo
donde los narcisos silvestres
se reflejaban
en un búcaro amarillo
de cristal, anunciándonos
posibles primaveras.

But no, it's still early.

And in the half-light of this room
that sleeps and dreams
of us,
the light of dawn breathes
filtering
through the gaps in this blind
when day breaks.

Naming the objects—coat rack,
light bulb, crucifix, books … mirror
where the wild daffodils
were reflected
on a yellow glass
vase, announcing
likely springs for us.

Amor
volverán
jardines cercados de mayo
bosques lavados de agua
para tu regreso.

Embriagándonos entonces
el sol incandescente
y la menta.

Yo seguiré buscando nieve en la cumbre
con que cubrir
la negra nostalgia del carbón
encendido sobre tu pubis.

My love,
gardens fenced in by May
water-washed woods
will come back
for your return.

We'll be enraptured then
by a white hot sun
and mint.

I will keep on searching on the peak for snow
to cover
the black nostalgia of coal
burning on your pubis.

Hemos hecho de nuestros momentos
un sacramento eterno
una bendición.

Nos hemos santiguado
con el agua de los charcos
y hemos besado
huracanes,
almendros,
dioses.

Sobre nuestros cuerpos
han crecido dolores como hospitales
de frío zinc
tribulaciones,
barcos en mares inmensos a la deriva
angustias
y fúnebres mantos de mártires
con puñales clavados
entre sus pechos.

We have turned our minutes
into an eternal sacrament
a blessing.

We have crossed ourselves
with puddle water
and have kissed
hurricanes,
almond trees,
gods.

On our body
have grown pains like hospitals
of cold zinc
tribulations,
ships in vast seas drifting
anguish
and funeral cloaks of martyrs
with daggers thrust
between their breast.

También hemos enjuagado
nuestros corazones
en abluciones de lejía,
en el silencioso almacén
de la niebla y el llanto.

We have also rinsed out
our hearts
in ablutions of bleach,
in the silent warehouse
of mist and sobbing.

… Después volver al inicio

y seguir

amortajando el hueco efímero
de los deseos.

–Amor cero–

El recuerdo.

Arrojar el olor de las flores marchitas
contra el oleaje del tiempo.

Nunca volver a despertarnos.

Y ver
nuestra mirada
tropezando
entre la espuma de los acantilados.

… Let us later return to the start

and continue

shrouding the ephemeral vacuity
of desires.

—Love zero—

The memory.

Let us throw the scent of withered flowers
against the swell of time.

Let us never wake up again.

And see
our gaze
tumbling
amid the foam of the cliffs.

No quisiera convertir esta noche
en una larga pesadilla.

Y cuando abra los ojos
seguir paseando
por la hectárea de tu piel
de tu hoguera.

Ver tu fotografía oxidada
en el viejo portarretratos
y ser
en tu rostro, ahora, la sonrisa
y la mirada
de aquellos días de verano
que nos bañaron
entre escamas de luz brillante
y los labios azules de las aguas
adonde llegaban flotando
los cuerpos pálidos de los ahogados.

I'd hate to turn this night
into a long nightmare.

And when I open my eyes
I'd keep on strolling
the hectare of your skin
of your bonfire.

I'd see your rusty photograph
in its old frame
and I'd exist
in your face, now, the smile
and the gaze
of those summer days
that bathed us
amid flakes of brilliant light
and the blue lips of the waters
to where the pale bodies
of the drowned arrived floating.

–Solo las postales de parques otoñales
y estanques con hojas secas
pueden entregarse
a un tiempo sepia
a una realidad virada–

—Only the postcards of parks in the fall
and ponds with dry leaves
can succumb
to a sepia time
to a skewed reality—

Pero el amor
es más intenso
que cualquiera de los tiempos.

–Más fuerte que la propia muerte–

Y nosotros
viajaremos este próximo atardecer
hasta el lejano país
que se esconde
del otro lado
de la raya última del horizonte.

But love
is more intense
than any of times.

—Stronger than death itself—

And we
will travel this next evening
toward the distant country
that is hidden
on the other side
of the last streak of the horizon.

Somieres ruidosos,
colchones viejos de lana blanca
han ocultado
el ritmo lúgubre de nuestro cántico.

La vida.

Caja de marfil
que celosamente guarda
el secreto tácito del amor.

Noisy bedsprings,
old mattresses of white wool
have concealed
the mournful rhythm of our song.

Life.

An ivory box
that jealously guards
the tacit secret of love.

A veces el interminable diálogo
de la noche
sin fin.

Sometimes the incessant dialogue
of night
without end.

A nuestra ventana ladraban
rabiosos los perros
con sus lenguas de hielo rojo
el triste aullido del abandono.

En la oscuridad.

At our window the dogs
were barking madly
with their tongues of red ice
the sad howl of abandonment.

In the darkness.

Tiemblan las llamas de las velas
el cansancio apagado.
La calma
de nuestros músculos.

La derrota.

Los golpes secos
de las hachas partiendo
los troncos del invierno.

Y la luz

izándose
por un mástil de heridas
como estandarte del dolor.

Ondeando
al viento, otro día más.

–Entonces ella recordará
su mejor boda
la demencia blanca
la muerte tranquila–

La desnudez próxima.

Y todo será el sueño de un sueño.

The candles' flames quiver
a quiet exhaustion.
The calm
of our muscles.

Our defeat.

The sharp blows
of axes cutting
logs for wintertime.

And light

hoisting
to a pole of wounds
like a banner of pain.

Fluttering
in the wind, one more day.

—Then she'll remember
her best wedding
the white lunacy
the quiet death—

The close nakedness.

And everything will be a dream within a dream.

La exactitud de los silencios.
Ese preciso instante.

Atmósfera
donde nada ocurre.

Callamos.
Apretamos el embozo de la colcha
con nuestros dedos, esperando
a quién pertenece
la primera palabra.

El primer verbo.

The accuracy of silences.
That very moment.

An atmosphere
where nothing happens.

We're quiet.
We hold the bedspread turndown
with our fingers, awaiting
to hear who is first
to speak.

Whose is the first word.

Y sueño
el sueño

de ser un cadáver olvidado
por la muerte.

Dormir

para despertar
lo que será luego recuerdo
o memoria escarbada
por los gallos al amanecer.

–En los almanaques de la casa,
pasaban los días
desvaneciéndose sus hojas.
Ecuaciones fugaces de alegría
más tarde
engendraban tristeza
y se multiplicaba
en rostros
que la serpiente de estrellas
nos dibujaba
en el interior de la retina–

And I dream
the dream

of being a corpse forgotten
by death.

To sleep

so as to awaken
what will be later recalled
or memory delved
by the dawn roosters.

—In the house's calendars
the days passed
shedding their leaves.
Fleeting equations of joy
later
engendered sadness
and it multiplied
on faces
that the serpent of stars
drew for us
inside our retina—

Voy surgiendo del agotamiento
como flor que brota
entre el ciénago
de las aguas estancadas
iniciando la primavera.

¿Pero, se coagula amarilla la sangre
en este cuerpo de invierno
que se apresura
al olvido?

... Podías morir esta noche un poco
deshabitándote.

Sabes que sobre tu boca
yo pondría
un océano blando de miel.

Todos mis siglos, bien despacio,
uno a uno
entre las aldeas
apagadas del alma de tu pecho.

Una corona encendida de abejas
alrededor de tu cuello
entre el cansancio de tu almohada
y la eterna guadaña
que nos amenaza.

I am slowly raising from exhaustion
like a flower that blooms
in the quagmire
of stagnant water
initiating spring.

But does blood coagulate yellow
in this winter body
that is pushed
toward oblivion?

… You could die this night a little
vacating yourself.

You know that on your mouth
I would lay
a tender ocean of honey.

All my centuries, rather slowly,
one by one,
amid muffled
hamlets of your breast's soul.

A crown burning with bees
around your neck
between the weariness of your pillow
and the eternal scythe
that threatens us.

Pero tú bien sabes
amor
que después vendrá
la ciega edad
a igualarnos a todos
en silencio, en muerte.

But you well know,
love,
that blind age
will come later
to make us all the same
in silence, in death.

Comulgamos
con el álbum redondo y triste de la noche.
Es nuestra prisión.

El pacto sellado con aliento
y versos como barrotes de metal
o lluvia oblicua
resbalando
por nuestros huesos.

Por la esfera del mundo.

Mi amor entre renglones.

¡Cómo nos hemos perdido
entre la profundidad de los signos
y los lenguajes!

We take communion
with the round and sad album of night.
It is our prison.

The pact sealed with breath
and verses like metal bars
or oblique rain
slipping
along our bones.

Through the sphere of the world.

My love between notebook lines.

How we got lost
amid the depth of signs
and languages!

Tu voz está gastada.
Tus palabras.

El dolor de tu lengua se hace mío
en este pozo
que se hunde hasta el corazón.

Esperamos dormidos
bajo el filo de la navaja
maullándonos al oído los gatos.

Todo se derrite en mis labios
ese olor intenso de lo que fue verano
ruda en floración tus muslos.

En ti, mi amor,
cobra el mercurio
la temperatura del deseo.

Your voice is worn out.
Your words.

The pain in your tongue becomes mine
in this pit
which sinks down to the heart.

We wait asleep
under the razor's edge
with the cats meowing at us.

Everything melts on my lips
that intense smell of what was summer
your thighs, rue in flowering.

In you, my love,
mercury reaches
the temperature of desire.

Ya no te veo.

Este frío húmedo
empaña los cristales
de la ventana de la habitación
que pronto quedará vacía.

No hay duda
solo el duradero calambre del dolor.

La pena y la fiebre.

I can't see you anymore.

This humid cold
mists up
the window panes of this room
that will soon be empty.

There is no doubt
only the hard cramp of grief.

Pain and fever.

La maleza ha crecido en los andenes
adueñándose del óxido
de aquellos raíles de infinito hierro
que nos llevaron un día
hasta el vocerío otoñal de los mercados.

Llegábamos
para examinarnos en amaneceres.

Entre acero de herramientas,
madera o mimbre,
cestas con aves, loza,
pescados en cajas de tabla
con hielo picado sobre verdes helechos
y otros colores
vendiéndose
en los puestos de fruta y hortalizas.

… Y el lejano olor a ultramar
perfumaba la piel.

Weeds have grown on the platforms
taking over the rust
of those rails of infinite iron
that took us one day
to the fall uproar of markets.

We arrived
to be tested on dawns.

Amid the steel of tools,
timber or willow,
baskets with birds, crockery,
fish in wooden crates
with crushed ice on green ferns
and other colors
being sold
on fruit and vegetable stalls.

… And the remote smell of overseas
perfumed our skin.

Uncidos al crepuscular yugo de la tarde
en urdimbre silenciosa
entre hojas de árboles
despojándose
de sus espumas más doradas
contemplábamos
el agonizar del día.

Puntual llegaba.

Después todos los olvidos.
Tras los cristales.

Bound to the twilight yoke of evening
in a silent warp
amid leaves of trees
stripping
of their most golden froth
we gazed at
the dying of day.

It arrived on time.

Later on, all oblivions.
Behind the windows.

Volvíamos por la senda
donde crecen
el beleño y la achicoria.

La tórtola zureaba nuestro caminar.

Entre el ramaje de los álamos
umbríos y oscuros
pasos de nómada
descubriendo el suicidio
de nuestras carnes desnudas.
Su inocencia vegetal de pétalo
a cada paso que dábamos…

Y el vuelo incierto de la libélula
en un zenit que trenzaba
su luz mortecina
a los juncos del río.

Raíces creciendo en nuestras manos
la piedra dentro del agua.

El mugido húmedo de las terneras
entre el verdor de los pastos
y el añil del cielo.

We returned across the path
where the henbane and the chicory
grow.

The turtledove cooed our walking.

Amid the branches of the poplars
shady and dark
the steps of a nomad
revealing the suicide
of our naked flesh.
Its plant-innocence of a petal
with every step we took …

And the uncertain flight of the dragonfly
in a zenith that braided
its faint light
to the reeds of the river.

Roots growing in our hands
the stone inside the water.

The wet mooing of calves
amid the greenness of pasture
and the indigo of the sky.

Llegan de lejos.

Con un ramo de espinos
respirando la noche.
El poso de sangre antigua
que aún habita en su paladar.

Llegan de lejos.

Sollozan
ante los miembros mutilados
y no apuran la última copa.

Son ellos.

–La carcoma se apodera
de nuestros sentidos
la carcoma se apodera
de un tiempo nuestro
y solo nuestro–

They arrive from afar.

With a branch of hawthorn
breathing the night.
The trace of ancient blood
that still dwells on their palate.

They arrive from afar.

They sob
before their mutilated limbs
but won't drink up the last cup.

It is them.

—Anxiety seizes
our senses
anxiety seizes
a time of ours
and ours only—

Ya va siendo tarde.
Pero podemos saborear juntos
el hinojo empapado un día
por el agua de las tormentas.

Los ángulos del invierno
desfalleciendo
ahora en nuestros labios.

It is getting late.
But together we can savor
the fennel soaked one day
by the water of storms.

The angles of winter
weakening
now on our lips.

Y el pulso secreto de tu cuerpo
me conforta
en el abrazo furtivo
de esta invernal isla blanca
del amor y la memoria.

And the secret pulse of your body
comforts me
in the furtive embrace
of this white winter island
of love and memory.

Así te quiero
para siempre
amor.

Reciente en mi memoria.

Como pan temprano
que llevarme a la boca
cada amanecer.

Thus I love you
forever
love.

Fresh in my memory.

Like early bread
I bring to my mouth
every dawn.

… Porque cada amanecer
somos
ese poema nuevo
que camina dando tumbos
hacia la muerte.

Una larga epístola nocturna
en voz baja.

Cuando llega el día
y su luz
nos condena
y nos salva de la nada.

En el prólogo blanco del inicio.
En el epílogo negro del final.

Álgebra del silencio y tinta derramada
en las lagunas del vacío.

… Because every dawn
we are
that new poem
that staggers
towards death.

A whispered
long night epistle.

When day breaks
and its light
condemns us
and saves us from nothing.

In the beginning's white prologue.
In the ending's black epilogue.

Algebra of silence and spilled ink
in the lacunae of emptiness.

Un paréntesis que se cierra
entre la carne ardiendo del amor.

Un paréntesis que se cierra
entre las cifras quebradas del tiempo.

Un paréntesis azotándonos
con un látigo de saliva en los ojos
nublándonos la vida, la mirada.

Como la fuerza de los imanes
cerrándonos
la poca sombra que nos queda
de la respiración.

A bracket closing
amid love's burning flesh.

A bracket closing
amid time's cracked figures.

A bracket flogging
our eyes with a whip of saliva,
clouding our life, our gaze.

Like the strength of magnets
closing
as little shade that is left
of our breathing.

Gotea impasible la cera
en crepúsculos de hachones encendidos.

Entre muros sagrados
y huellas de abril
por calles mojadas.

Habita la memoria en el salmo de sus esquinas.

El umbral. La penumbra.

Y muere la muerte en el amor.

En perlados lechos.
En estameña cálida.

Y la mirada celeste
es ahora un océano distante
un océano herido
por el rocío de la mañana.

Wax drips impassively
in twilights of burning firebrands.

Amid holy walls
and signs of April
through wet streets.

Memory dwells in the psalm of its corners.

The threshold. The half-light.

And death dies into love.

In pearled beds.
In warm serge.

And the heavenly gaze
is now a distant ocean
an ocean wounded
by morning dew.

Los visillos cubren los cristales de la galería.

¿Qué existe dentro?

Hogar sin nadie.

… Si la tarde nos entierra
bajo una luz de arena y cactus.

Bajo la luz aterida
de un final de invierno.

Y la gente camina gris por las avenidas.
Los pájaros tienen insectos
en sus picos de fuego.

The lace curtains cover the balcony windows.

What exists inside?

A home with no one.

… If the evening should bury us
under a light of sand and cactus.

Under the frozen light
of a winter's end.

And people trudge gray along the avenues.
The birds hold insects
in their beaks of fire.

La belleza tampoco es verdad.

La belleza es una sortija
de diamantes ensangrentados
en alianza con el tiempo
que nos pudre el corazón oculto
el espíritu visible, el excremento.

Ahora la belleza
se aloja
en el triste imperio de la muerte
donde azota el viento
y se quiebra el espejo.

Donde se dibuja
en la ruina
la sombra.

Su caricia quemando
las rocas, el musgo, los puñales o las ingles.

No hay gargantas
que hagan crujir otros silencios.

Beauty is not truth either.

Beauty is a ring
of diamonds covered in blood
wedded with the time
that rots our concealed hearts
our visible spirits, excrements.

Now beauty
abides
at the dismal empire of death
where the wind lashes
and the mirror cracks.

Where the shadow
is outlined
on the ruins.

Her caress burning
rocks, moss, daggers or groins.

There are no throats
that make other silences creak.

Vamos hacia el palacio desnudo
donde reside la nada.

El secreto de la existencia.
La soledad de quien espera partir
y entonar
su hora última.

Su canción más triste del alma.

¿Acaso, era esto la vida?

We are headed for the bare palace
where nothingness dwells.

The secret of existence.
The solitude of him who expects to leave
and sing
his time.

His saddest song of the soul.

Was this life, by any chance?

Pisada está la flor de la mandrágora
y la hermosura de su fruto
se deshace en la boca.

Mastico silencio
como quien mastica la mentira
y los toros beben campos de nieve.

Es probable que lleguen
otros cielos sin estrellas
otros mares sin agua
donde ceñir
nuestras cinturas de sal
con algas y espinas
de peces transparentes.

Y descansar.

Descansar de tanta muerte
en bancales de niebla
o collados
de agotada luz.

The flower of the mandrake is trodden
and the beauty of its fruit
melts in my mouth.

I chew silence
like someone chewing a lie
and bulls drink fields of snow.

It's likely that other starless skies
may come
other waterless seas
girding
our salty waists
with algae and bones
of transparent fish.

And to rest.

To rest from so much death
on terraces of fog
or hillocks
of exhausted light.

Somos un sable púrpura
en la noche que se avecina.

Somos sangre ajada.

El mosto que fermenta los labios
de lo que tanto se amó.

Somos vísceras y terciopelo
sobre los líquenes del mundo.

Somos la frente ebúrnea
donde atardecen racimos podridos
de fruta abrasada por los hielos.

Somos el bostezar largo
entre los muslos tiernos del sueño.

Somos la plata oscura de los muertos.

Somos el mármol consumido
donde descansa la inscripción.

Los días iniciados
los que ya no tienen fin…

We are a purple saber
in the approaching night.

We are worn-out blood.

The must that ferments the lips
of what we used to love dearly.

We are viscera and velvet
on the lichens of the world.

We are the ivory brow
where the rotten clusters of fruit
parched by ice grow late.

We are the long yawning
amid the soft thighs of sleep.

We are the darkened silver of the dead.

We are the shrunk marble
where the inscription rests.

The started days,
those now with no end …

Ahora que ya no estamos
siendo tú,
la ceniza que arrastrará los vientos.

Yo, esa piedra que tiembla
como un pábilo encendido
sobre la tierra.

Ahora que ya no estamos
la luz se filtra, lenta
por las vidrieras del alma.

Es un bodegón de cantos.
Una urna con incienso.
Un cofre abierto de arco iris
de voces.

Un animal que brama
entre las cuerdas templadas de un arpa
y su gemido
atraviesa el invierno.

Va hacia nunca.

Now that we are no longer
being you,
the ash that will sweep the winds.

I, that stone trembling
like a wick that burns
over the earth.

Now that we are no longer here
light filters, slowly
through the windows of the soul.

It is a still life of pebbles.
An urn with incense.
An open chest of a rainbow
of voices.

An animal bellowing
between a harp's tuned stings
and its whine
cuts through winter.

It is never-bound.

Hacia nunca.

Cruzando puentes
por donde los años
pasaban amontonados.

Bosques de resina o de ámbar
donde nuestro amor
crepitaba en llamas.

Se hacía incendio.

Ahora que ya no estamos
ni tan siquiera los días
nos besaron
montañas en la boca
ni néctar en las lenguas.

Ahora que ya no estamos.

¿Qué ábaco se equivocó?

Never-bound.

Crossing bridges
where the years
passed piled up.

Woods of resin or amber
where our love
crackled in flames.

It became a fire.

Now that we are no longer here
not even the days
kissed us
mountains on our mouths
nor nectar on our tongues.

Now that we are no longer here.

What abacus was wrong?

Ahora que ya no estamos.

¿Acaso, era esto la vida?

¿esa orquídea pisoteada
entre la arcilla espesa
que nos deja el tiempo
con sus huellas
bajo una luz
descuartizada?

¿o era, ese mineral precioso
que brilla y reluce
en los escaparates de las joyerías
para quedar después sepultado
entre el estiércol de las cuadras?

Ahora que ya no estamos.

¿Acaso, amor, era esto la vida?

Now that we are no longer here.

Was this life, by any chance?

That trampled orchid
in the thick clay
left by time
with its tracks
under a quartered
light?

Or was it that precious mineral
that sparkles and shines
in jewelry store windows
and is later buried
in the manure of stables?

Now that we are no longer here.

Was this life, by any chance, my love?

About the Author

Jesús Losada (Zamora, 1962) is the author of eleven collections of poetry, among them *Huerto cerrado del amor* (2nd prize, Premio Adonáis, 1994), *La noche del funambulista* (Premio Provincia, 1998), and *Corazón frontera* (Premio "San Juan de la Cruz", 2010). He has over twenty years of professional management in cultural events and academic experience. He holds a PhD in Spanish and Portuguese Philology, as well as a BA in Romance Languages.

About the Translators

Michael Smith (Dublin, 1942) is a poet whose *Collected Poems* was published in 2009. His translations, many in collaboration with Luis Ingelmo, of Spanish and Latin American poets are numerous and have been critically acclaimed. The latest collection of his own poems, *Prayers for the Dead & Other Poems*, appeared in 2014. He is a member of Aosdána, the Irish National Academy of Artists.

Luis Ingelmo (Palencia, 1970) holds degrees in English Philology and Philosophy. He spent seven years in the USA. His cotranslations with Michael Smith include the poems of Elsa Cross, Claudio Rodríguez and Aníbal Núñez, among many others. His translations into Spanish include works by Thomas MacGreevy, Wole Soyinka, Natasha Trethewey and Derek Walcott. He is the author of the book of short tales, *La métrica del olvido* [The Metrics of Oblivion], and a poetry collection, *Aguapié* [Pomace Wine].

Free Verse Editions

Edited by Jon Thompson

13 ways of happily by Emily Carr
Between the Twilight and the Sky by Jennie Neighbors
Blood Orbits by Ger Killeen
The Bodies by Chris Sindt
The Book of Isaac by Aidan Semmens
Canticle of the Night Path by Jennifer Atkinson
Child in the Road by Cindy Savett
Condominium of the Flesh by Valerio Magrelli, translated by Clarissa Botsford
Contrapuntal by Christopher Kondrich
Country Album by James Capozzi
The Curiosities by Brittany Perham
Current by Lisa Fishman
Dismantling the Angel by Eric Pankey
Divination Machine by F. Daniel Rzicznek
Erros by Morgan Lucas Schuldt
The Forever Notes by Ethel Rackin
The Flying House by Dawn-Michelle Baude
Instances: Selected Poems by Jeongrye Choi, translated by Brenda Hillman, Wayne de Fremery, and Jeongrye Choi
The Magnetic Brackets by Jesús Losada, translated by Michael Smith and Luis Ingelmo
A Map of Faring by Peter Riley
No Shape Bends the River So Long by Monica Berlin and Beth Marzoni
Pilgrimly by Siobhan Scarry
Physis by Nicolas Pesque, translated by Cole Swensen
Poems from above the Hill & Selected Work by Ashur Etwebi, translated by Brenda Hillman and Diallah Haidar
The Prison Poems by Miguel Hernández, translated by Michael Smith
Puppet Wardrobe by Daniel Tiffany
Quarry by Carolyn Guinzio
remanence by Boyer Rickel
Signs Following by Ger Killeen
Split the Crow by Sarah Sousa
Summoned by Guillevic, translated by Monique Chefdor
Sunshine Wound by L. S. Klatt

These Beautiful Limits by Thomas Lisk
An Unchanging Blue: Selected Poems 1962–1975 by Rolf Dieter Brinkmann, translated by Mark Terrill
Under the Quick by Molly Bendall
Verge by Morgan Lucas Schuldt
The Wash by Adam Clay
We'll See by George Godeau, translated by Kathleen McGookey
What Stillness Illuminated by Yermiyahu Ahron Taub
Winter Journey [Viaggio d'inverno] by Attilio Bertolucci, translated by Nicholas Benson
Wonder Rooms by Allison Funk

www.ingramcontent.com/pod-product-compliance
Ingram Content Group UK Ltd.
Pitfield, Milton Keynes, MK11 3LW, UK
UKHW041643190726
13854UKWH00006B/2675